STAR WARS™

A NEW HOPE

THE 40TH ANNIVERSARY

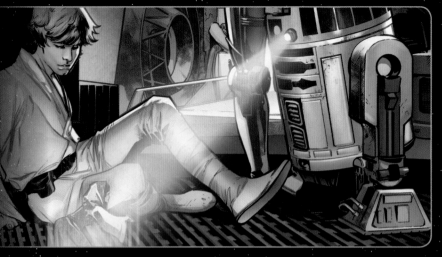

STAR WARS™

A NEW HOPE

THE 40ᵀᴴ ANNIVERSARY

WRITTEN BY

JESS HARROLD

STAR WARS 40TH ANNIVERSARY VARIANT PROGRAM EDITOR

HEATHER ANTOS

COVER ART BY

GREG LAND & JUSTIN PONSOR AND ADI GRANOV

COLLECTION EDITOR **JEFF YOUNGQUIST**
ASSISTANT EDITOR **CAITLIN O'CONNELL**
ASSOCIATE MANAGING EDITOR **KATERI WOODY**
ASSOCIATE MANAGER, DIGITAL ASSETS **JOE HOCHSTEIN**
SENIOR EDITOR, SPECIAL PROJECTS **JENNIFER GRÜNWALD**
EDITOR, SPECIAL PROJECTS **MARK D. BEAZLEY**
SVP PRINT, SALES & MARKETING **DAVID GABRIEL**

EDITOR IN CHIEF **C.B. CEBULSKI**
CHIEF CREATIVE OFFICER **JOE QUESADA**
PRESIDENT **DAN BUCKLEY**

SPECIAL THANKS TO **JORDAN D. WHITE**,
JACQUE PORTE, **AVIA PEREZ** & **ELISSA HUNTER**

STAR WARS: A NEW HOPE — THE 40TH ANNIVERSARY. First printing 2018. ISBN 978-1-302-91128-7. Published by MARVEL WORLDWIDE, INC., a subsidiary of MARVEL ENTERTAINMENT, LLC. OFFICE OF PUBLI-CATION: 135 West 50th Street, New York, NY 10020. STAR WARS and related text and illustrations are trademarks and/or copyrights, in the United States and other countries, of Lucasfilm Ltd. and/or its affiliates. © & TM Lucasfilm Ltd. No similarity between any of the names, characters, persons, and/or institutions in this magazine with those of any living or dead person or institution is intended, and any such similarity which may exist is purely coincidental. Marvel and its logos are TM Marvel Characters, Inc. **Printed in China.** DAN BUCKLEY, President, Marvel Entertainment; JOE QUESADA, Chief Creative Officer; TOM BREVOORT, SVP of Publishing; DAVID BOGART, SVP of Business Affairs & Operations, Publishing & Partnership; DAVID GABRIEL, SVP of Sales & Marketing, Publishing; JEFF YOUNGQUIST, VP of Production & Special Projects; DAN CARR, Executive Director of Publishing Technology; ALEX MORALES, Director of Publishing Operations; SUSAN CRESPI, Production Manager; STAN LEE, Chairman Emeritus. For information regarding advertising in Marvel Comics or on Marvel.com, please contact Jonathan Parkhideh, VP of Digital Media & Marketing Solutions, at jparkhideh@marvel.com. For Marvel subscription inquiries, please call 888-511-5480. **Manufactured between 12/1/2017 and 2/12/2018 by R.R. DONNELLEY ASIA PRINTING SOLUTIONS, CHINA.**

10 9 8 7 6 5 4 3 2 1

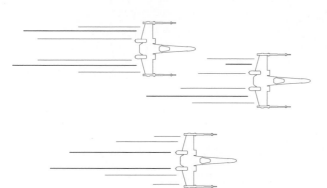

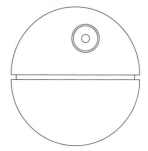

Star Wars and Marvel

It's an association that goes right back to the beginning—all the way to the summer of 1977, when a certain movie changed the world...and an eye-catching comic book leapt off the racks. "Enter: Luke Skywalker!" the bold cover proclaimed. "Will he **save** the galaxy -- or **destroy** it?"

Four decades on, the Marvel/*Star Wars* connection is stronger than ever. So what better way to honor the 40th anniversary of *Star Wars*: Episode IV *A New Hope* than through the unique art form of the comic-book cover? Over the pages that follow, 48 variant covers from Marvel's *Star Wars* titles—drawn by some of the industry's most talented artists—tell the story of *A New Hope*, scene by iconic scene. An accompanying narrative guides you through the film's events, while sketches and work-in-progress artwork demonstrate how each illustrator approached the task of reinterpreting a famous motion-picture sequence in a single image. A bonus cover gallery and other additional content further celebrate the relationship of Marvel and *Star Wars*, past and present.

You probably know what happens—but you've never seen it unfold like this. And if you're one of the few still wondering exactly what Luke Skywalker has in store for the galaxy, well, you're in for a treat.

May the Force be with you—and Make Yours Marvel!

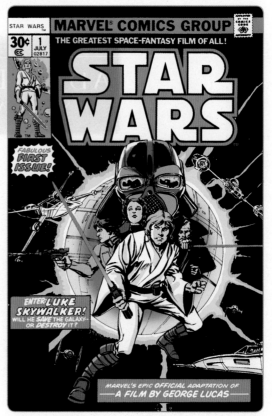

STAR WARS (1977) #1 COVER BY **HOWARD CHAYKIN** & **TOM PALMER**

A long time ago in a galaxy far, far away....

IT IS A PERIOD OF CIVIL WAR...

Rebel spaceships, striking from a hidden base, have won their first victory against the evil Galactic Empire. During the battle, Rebel spies managed to steal secret plans to the Empire's ultimate weapon, the Death Star—an armored space station with enough power to destroy an entire planet. Pursued by the Empire's sinister agents, Princess Leia races home aboard her starship, custodian of the stolen plans that can save her people and restore freedom to the galaxy....

"WE'RE DOOMED. THERE'LL BE NO ESCAPE FOR THE PRINCESS THIS TIME." — C-3PO

Captured by an Imperial Star Destroyer, Princess Leia's vessel is boarded by the Empire's ruthless enforcer, Darth Vader, and his squadron of stormtroopers. Panicked protocol droid C-3PO seeks to avoid enemy fire, but loses track of his friend, R2-D2. C-3PO catches up to R2-D2 just as Leia seizes the opportunity to hide the plans in the unassuming-looking astromech droid. Can anyone out there in the galaxy help her in her plight?

STAR WARS: POE DAMERON #10 **STUART IMMONEN**

While Vader and his stormtroopers scour the ship for the Death Star plans, C-3PO reluctantly agrees to follow R2-D2 into an escape pod. They blast off together on what R2-D2 claims is a "secret mission"— and all hope now lies with them.

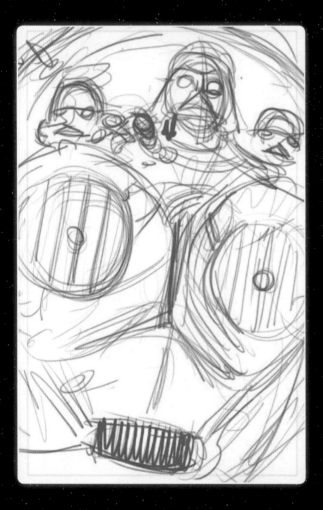

STAR WARS (2015) #27 **RYAN STEGMAN** & **JORDAN BOYD**

aptured by stormtroopers, Leia is brought before Vader and interrogated. While demands to know the location of the stolen plans, she insists she is merely a ember of the Imperial Senate on a diplomatic mission to Alderaan. He accuses er of being part of the Rebel Alliance and a traitor, and orders his men to take er away. The only possible answer is that the plans were hidden on the escape pod last seen hurtling toward the desert planet Tatooine.

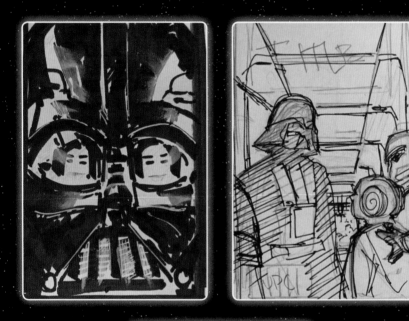

"WE SEEM TO BE MADE TO SUFFER— IT'S OUR LOT IN LIFE." — C-3PO

As they wander through the desert, C-3PO loses patience with "near-sighted scrap-pile" R2-D2 and his so-called mission. The bickering droids go their separate ways, yet both fall victim to the scavenger race of Jawas. They are reunited as captives aboard the Jawas' droid-filled sandcrawler, and together they face an uncertain fate: Will they be broken up for parts or, even worse, melted down as scrap?

JAWAS SEIZE R2-D2 IN *STAR WARS* (1977) #1 • ART BY **HOWARD CHAYKIN** & **MARIE SEVERIN**

STAR WARS: POE DAMERON #11 **MICHAEL WALSH**

"THAT R2 UNIT IS IN PRIME CONDITION— A REAL BARGAIN." — C-3PO

The profit-hungry Jawas bring their wares to the home of moisture farmer Owen Lars, who is in the market for a good droid or two. C-3PO offers assurances that there's more to him than protocol and etiquette, convincing Owen he will have no problem understanding the binary language of moisture evaporators. The farmer tells his nephew, Luke Skywalker, to clean up C-3PO and his chosen astromech, R5-D4—but when it malfunctions, C-3PO persuades Luke that R2-D2 is a first-class alternative.

STAR WARS: DARTH MAUL (2017) #1 **TERRY DODSON** & **RACHEL DODSON**

**"HELP ME, OBI-WAN KENOBI—
YOU'RE MY ONLY HOPE."** — PRINCESS LEIA

As Luke voices his frustrations at being trapped on a "rock" of a planet,
he is fascinated to hear of C-3PO's involvement in the Rebellion. And while
cleaning R2-D2, the young farmboy makes an incredible discovery: a fragment
of a holographic recording left by a beautiful woman. R2-D2 seeks to pass it
off as a malfunction to be ignored. Pressed by C-3PO, he reveals it is a private
message for an Obi-Wan Kenobi. Could it be, Luke wonders, that Obi-Wan
has some connection to the strange old hermit Ben Kenobi?

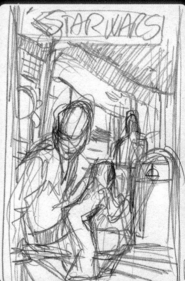

STAR WARS: DOCTOR APHRA #4 **PEPE LARRAZ** & **DAVID CURIEL**

> ## "LUKE'S JUST NOT A FARMER. HE HAS TOO MUCH OF HIS FATHER IN HIM."
> — AUNT BERU

Luke is eager to follow his friends, leave the farm behind and join the Imperial Academy, but his hopes are dashed by his uncle, who needs his help for one more season. Luke's Aunt Beru is sympathetic, but Owen is afraid to let him leave. Gazing out across Tatooine, Luke wonders whether he'll ever achieve his dreams and journey to the stars.

"SOMEONE WAS IN THE POD..."
— STORMTROOPER

Stormtroopers on lumbering dewbacks scour the surface of Tatooine and find the escape pod—as well as evidence that these are droids they're looking for. Meanwhile, unbeknownst to Luke, R2-D2 sneaks away from the farm. The headstrong droid is determined to find Obi-Wan Kenobi.

STAR WARS: DOCTOR APHRA #5 MARC LAMING & MATTHEW WILSON

"OBI-WAN KENOBI...NOW THAT'S A NAME I'VE NOT HEARD IN A LONG TIME." — BEN KENOBI

Luke and C-3PO catch up with R2-D2—just in time to come under attack from the deadly Tusken Raiders. A hooded figure scares away the primitive Sand People; as an unconscious Luke comes to, he recognizes the man as Ben Kenobi. When Luke asks Ben about Obi-Wan, the old man's answer is surprising: The one they seek isn't a relative, and he isn't dead—Ben is Obi-Wan Kenobi.

> "THIS IS THE WEAPON OF A JEDI KNIGHT. NOT AS CLUMSY OR RANDOM AS A BLASTER. AN ELEGANT WEAPON FOR A MORE CIVILIZED AGE." — OBI-WAN KENOBI

At Obi-Wan's home, the old man reveals he fought in the Clone Wars as a Jedi Knight—alongside Luke's father. Obi-Wan tells Luke his father was the best star pilot in the galaxy, a cunning warrior and a good friend—and that there's something he wanted his son to have. For the first time, Luke wields his father's lightsaber, and Obi-Wan tells the story of the Jedi Knights. For more than 1,000 generations, they were the guardians of peace and justice in the Old Republic, before the dark times of the Empire. But now the Jedi are all but extinct. Vader was once Obi-Wan's pupil, but was seduced by the dark side of the Force. Vader helped the Empire hunt down the Jedi, and betrayed and murdered Luke's father. The young farmboy is fascinated by tales of the Force—the energy field created by all living things that binds the galaxy together and gives the Jedi their powers.

"YOU MUST LEARN THE WAYS OF THE FORCE."
— OBI-WAN KENOBI

Before Obi-Wan can continue his story, he is interrupted by R2-D2, eager to complete his mission. Obi-Wan easily accesses the full holographic message left by Princess Leia. She says she had set out to bring Obi-Wan to her father, who the old Jedi had served during the Clone Wars. This is the Rebellion's most desperate hour, and information vital to its survival is hidden inside R2-D2. Leia's father will know how to retrieve it, but that means Obi-Wan must head to the planet Alderaan. Claiming to be too old for this sort of thing, Obi-Wan wants Luke to commence training so they can go to Alderaan together—but Luke feels the weight of obligation and must remain on his uncle's farm.

STAR WARS (2015) #30 **JAVIER RODRÍGUEZ**

As Imperial officers meet aboard the nearly fully operational Death Star, its commander, Grand Moff Tarkin, brings news that the Emperor has swept away the last remnants of the Old Republic. The galaxy now will be ruled by fear of the planet-destroying battle station. Admiral Motti boasts that the Death Star is now the ultimate power in the universe, and mocks Vader's "sorcerer's ways," which have so far failed to retrieve the stolen plans. In retaliation, the Dark Lord of the Sith offers a demonstration of the Force in action, choking Motti with but a gesture—only releasing him at the last moment at Tarkin's order.

STAR WARS: DOCTOR APHRA #6 **ROD REIS**

"I WANT TO LEARN THE WAYS OF THE FORCE AND BECOME A JEDI LIKE MY FATHER." — LUKE SKYWALKER

Returning home, an anguished Luke finds the farm destroyed—and the charred remains of his aunt and uncle. Realizing the stormtroopers must have tracked the droids there and killed his family, Luke's mind is made up. With nothing left for him on Tatooine, he will join Obi-Wan on his journey to Alderaan—and seek a new destiny as a Jedi.

"THESE AREN'T THE DROIDS YOU'RE LOOKING FOR."
— OBI-WAN KENOBI

To find a way offworld, Obi-Wan, Luke and the droids must first gain access to Mos Eisley spaceport. But with stormtroopers on the lookout for C-3PO and R2-D2, their way seems blocked—until Obi-Wan uses a Jedi mind trick to persuade the soldiers to let them through. The Force, he explains to Luke, can have a strong influence on the weak-minded.

...s Eisley cantina: where the drinks flow freely, all species are we... ...for droids—and the band plays on, no matter what. If you want... ...freighter pilot on Tatooine, this is the place to look. But be wa... ...things can get a little rough. It's best to be ready for anything.

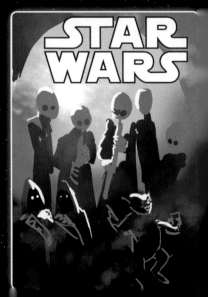

YOU'VE NEVER HEARD OF THE *MILLENNIUM FALCON?*
IT'S THE SHIP THAT MADE THE KESSEL RUN IN LESS
THAN 12 PARSECS." — HAN SOLO

Chewbacca the Wookiee introduces Obi-Wan and Luke to Han Solo, captain
of the *Millennium Falcon*. Han promises the *Falcon* is fast enough to keep
them clear of the Empire and get them to Alderaan—for a price. Obi-Wan
promises 2,000 credits up front and 15,000 on safe arrival—no questions
asked. With a bargain struck, they have themselves a ship. Han can't
believe his luck—this deal could really save his neck.

STAR WARS: DOCTOR APHRA #7 **GREG LAND** & **EDGAR DELGADO**

> **"JABBA'S PUT A PRICE ON YOUR HEAD SO LARGE EVERY BOUNTY HUNTER IN THE GALAXY WILL BE LOOKING FOR YOU."** — GREEDO

While Obi-Wan and Luke set out to raise funds, and Chewbacca leaves to ready the ship, Han's departure is interrupted by the bounty hunter Greedo, who holds him at gunpoint. Jabba the Hutt has grown tired of waiting for Han's debts to be cleared, and now there's a price on his head—one Greedo is looking to collect. Words alone can't get Han out of this one, and below the table his hand moves to his blaster. Shots are fired, but Greedo's is his last. The bounty hunter falls dead, and the sharpshooting smuggler makes a swift getaway.

Han arrives at the *Falcon*—but Jabba the Hutt is waiting for him. Ever the smart-talking smuggler, Han manages to negotiate extra time to pay in return for an additional 15 percent on his debt. But Jabba warns Han that if he crosses him again, there won't be a safe place left to hide in the galaxy.

"SHE MAY NOT LOOK LIKE MUCH, BUT SHE'S GOT IT WHERE IT COUNTS, KID." — HAN SOLO

It may seem like a piece of junk to Luke, but the *Falcon* takes flight with Han and Chewbacca at the controls—despite some last-minute blaster fire from pursuing stormtroopers. A jump to lightspeed quickly puts them beyond the reach of a pair of orbiting Star Destroyers, and their course is set for Alderaan.

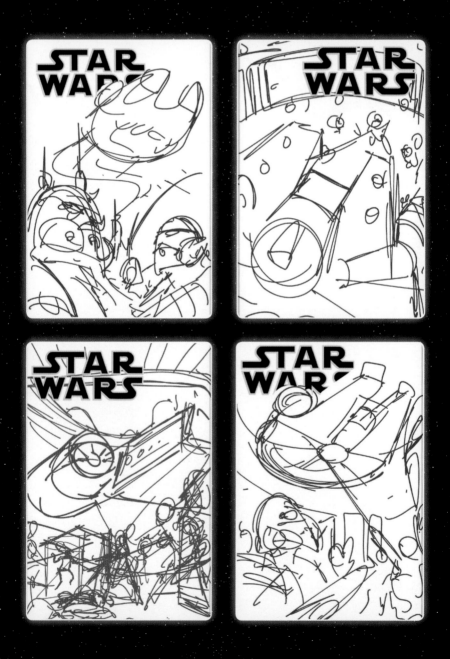

"HER RESISTANCE TO THE MIND PROBE IS FORMIDABLE." — DARTH VADER

Held captive on the Death Star, Leia is at the mercy of Vader and his interrogation droid—but the courageous princess refuses to divulge the location of the hidden rebel base.

STAR WARS: DOCTOR APHRA #8 **JEN BARTEL**

"I FELT A GREAT DISTURBANCE IN THE FORCE— AS IF MILLIONS OF VOICES SUDDENLY CRIED OUT IN TERROR, AND WERE SUDDENLY SILENCED."

— OBI-WAN KENOBI

As the Death Star destroys Alderaan, an anguished Obi-Wan Kenobi senses the terrible loss of life.

STAR WARS: DARTH MAUL (2017) #5 **JULIAN TOTINO TEDESCO**

"REMEMBER, A JEDI CAN FEEL THE FORCE FLOWING THROUGH HIM." — OBI-WAN KENOBI

Aboard the *Falcon*, Luke begins his lightsaber training. Obi-Wan encourages him to let go of his conscious self and act on instinct. Donning a helmet with the blast shield down, Luke is told to stretch out with his feelings—and is able to block the remote's shots. Despite Han's skepticism regarding the Force, Obi-Wan assures Luke he has taken his first step into a larger world.

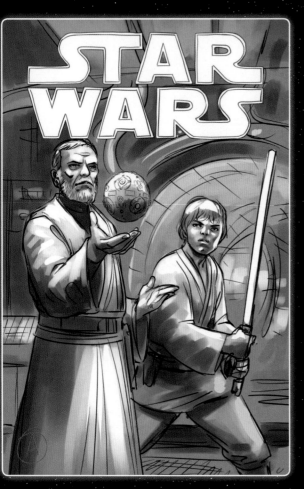

"THAT'S NO MOON..."

— OBI-WAN KENOBI

As the *Falcon* exits hyperspace into an uncharted meteor shower, Han arrives at
a terrifying realization: Alderaan has been destroyed, and this is all that remains.
The Falcon comes under fire from an Imperial fighter, but such a short-range
vessel shouldn't be this deep in space on its own. It seems to be heading for
a small moon, but the truth is far worse: The "moon" is a space station.
Before Han can take action, they're caught in a tractor beam—
and the *Falcon* is held in the Death Star's unrelenting grip.

STAR WARS: DOCTOR APHRA #9 **REILLY BROWN** & **JIM CHARALAMPIDIS**

"I SENSE SOMETHING— A PRESENCE I'VE NOT FELT SINCE..."

— DARTH VADER

The *Falcon* is pulled aboard the Death Star. With no sign of any crew or the droids they're seeking, Vader orders every part of the ship to be searched. The Sith Lord senses someone he knew long, long ago: his old master, Obi-Wan Kenobi.

STAR WARS: DOCTOR APHRA #10 **CASPAR WIJNGAARD**

"THE FORCE WILL BE WITH YOU, ALWAYS."
— OBI-WAN KENOBI

When the coast is clear, Han, Chewbacca, Luke, Obi-Wan, C-3PO and R2-D2 climb out of the secret compartment on the *Falcon* that Han uses for smuggling. They ambush a pair of stormtroopers, steal their armor and sneak out onto the Death Star. R2-D2 accesses the Imperial computer network, discovering how to disarm the tractor beam, and Obi-Wan sets out alone to act on that information. Luke is eager to join him, but Obi-Wan tells him to remain with the droids and fulfill their primary mission—his destiny lies along a different path.

THE CREW EMERGES FROM ITS HIDING PLACE IN *STAR WARS* (1977) #3 • ART BY **HOWARD CHAYKIN** & **STEVE LEIALOHA**

"I CAN'T SEE A THING IN THIS HELMET."
— LUKE SKYWALKER

R2-D2 learns Leia is being held on board and is scheduled to be executed. Luke is determined to rescue her, but Han is in no mood to be a hero—until Luke reveals that Leia is a rich and powerful princess, and that the reward for saving her would be bigger than even Han could imagine. Disguised as stormtroopers, and with Chewbacca posing as their prisoner, they set out for Leia's cell.

JKE, WE'RE GONNA HAVE COMPAN

— HAN SOLO

---

spicious Imperial forces stop them in a corridor, Chewbacca
and triggers a firefight. Han, Luke and Chewbacca defeat t
p of stormtroopers, but more soldiers will soon be on their

"AREN'T YOU A LITTLE SHORT FOR A STORMTROOPER?" — PRINCESS LEIA

Reaching Leia's cell, Luke is dumbstruck by the sight of her—only to have her tease him about his height. He removes his helmet and tells her he's Luke Skywalker, and that he's there to rescue her. Together, they set off to find Obi-Wan.

"THIS IS SOME RESCUE."
— PRINCESS LEIA

Luke and Leia unite with Han and Chewbacca. With their only escape route blocked, and under enemy fire, the princess shows she's no damsel in distress. Taking charge of the poorly thought-out rescue, she grabs Luke's blaster, returns fire on the stormtroopers and finds a way out for her allies—into the garbage chute.

LEIA TAKES ACTION IN *STAR WARS* (1977) #4 • ART BY **HOWARD CHAYKIN** & **STEVE LEIALOHA**

Leia, Han and Chewbacca find themselves in one of the Death
netrable, magnetically sealed trash compactors, up to their kne
and filthy water—and overwhelmed by the incredible smell. "It
offers Leia—and she's right. There's something else alive in th
monstrous creature grabs Luke with its tentacle and drags hir
s to rescue him fail, until suddenly the beast lets go and disap
ore the walls start closing in. As Han and Leia make a vain att
e walls with debris, Luke tries to contact C-3PO. And just befor
ed, R2-D2 manages to turn off the trash compactor and save tl

"GET BACK TO THE SHIP!"
— HAN SOLO

Luke, Leia, Han and Chewbacca make their return to the *Falcon*—but just as they get a glimpse of it from above, a squadron of stormtroopers blocks their way. Han charges into action, blaster in hand, and tells the others to get to the ship. His faithful friend, Chewbacca, follows him into battle—until, overwhelmed by numbers, they're forced into a hasty retreat, exchanging fire as they go.

STAR WARS (2015) #36 **ED McGUINNESS, MARK MORALES** & **LAURA MARTIN**

"WHAT WAS THAT?"
— STORMTROOPER

Meanwhile, Obi-Wan Kenobi stealthily makes his way through the Death Star and finds the crucial control center he needs to power down the tractor beam. He uses the Force to distract a pair of stormtroopers and make good his escape.

OBI-WAN KENOBI EVADES STORMTROOPERS IN *STAR WARS* (1977) #4 • ART BY **HOWARD CHAYKIN** & **STEVE LEIALOHA**

STAR WARS: DOCTOR APHRA #12 **NICK ROCHE** & **JORDAN BOYD**

"I THINK WE TOOK A WRONG TURN."
— LUKE SKYWALKER

Luke and Leia's escape route is blocked by a chasm too wide to leap.
As they come under fire, Luke closes the door behind them and blasts the
lock—giving them no choice but to somehow make their way across.
With stormtroopers closing in from above and behind, Luke uses a
grappling hook from his belt to swing himself and Leia to safety.

STAR WARS: POE DAMERON #19 **CHRIS SAMNEE** & **MATTHEW WILSON**

"WE MEET AGAIN AT LAST."

— DARTH VADER

Obi-Wan comes face-to-face with Vader. Each draws his lightsaber and prepares for battle. For the Dark Lord of the Sith, the circle is now complete: Once, he was Obi-Wan's pupil; now, he will demonstrate that he is the master. Enduring Vader's taunts, Obi-Wan battles long enough to draw the stormtroopers guarding the Falcon away from their post, clearing the way for Luke, Leia, Han, Chewbacca, C-3PO and R2-D2 to reach the ship.

STAR WARS: JEDI OF THE REPUBLIC — MACE WINDU #2 **ADI GRANOV**

"IF YOU STRIKE ME DOWN, I SHALL BECOME MORE POWERFUL THAN YOU CAN POSSIBLY IMAGINE." — OBI-WAN KENOBI

Seeing Luke, Obi-Wan realizes his moment has arrived. He raises his lightsaber and quietly submits. Vader strikes the killing blow, and Luke screams in grief for his friend. Obi-Wan disappears, his robes falling to the floor. Luke's first thought is of revenge, but Obi-Wan's voice in his head implores him to run for the ship.

"GREAT, KID! DON'T GET COCKY."

— HAN SOLO

Under fire, the rebels make their way aboard the *Falcon* and blast off, pursued by a fleet of TIE fighters. With Chewbacca at the controls, Han and Luke head to the gun wells. The *Falcon* takes some hits, just about holding together, while some sharpshooting from Han and an excited Luke dispatches the last of the enemy. The crew safely makes the jump into hyperspace—but Vader has planted a homing beacon on their ship.

The *Falcon* arrives at the rebel base on the moon Yavin 4, where Leia and General Dodonna access the stolen Death Star plans. Dodonna briefs his pilots on the heavily shielded space station, which has more firepower than half the Starfleet. But it also has a weakness. The Death Star's defenses are designed to thwart a direct, large-scale assault—but a small, one-man fighter should be able to penetrate them. The approach, however, will be difficult. And the target—a thermal exhaust port—is only two meters wide. Hit that target with a proton torpedo, and it will travel down the shaft directly to the reactor system. A precise hit will start a chain reaction that should destroy the station. But surely that's impossible, even for a computer? Not according to Luke.

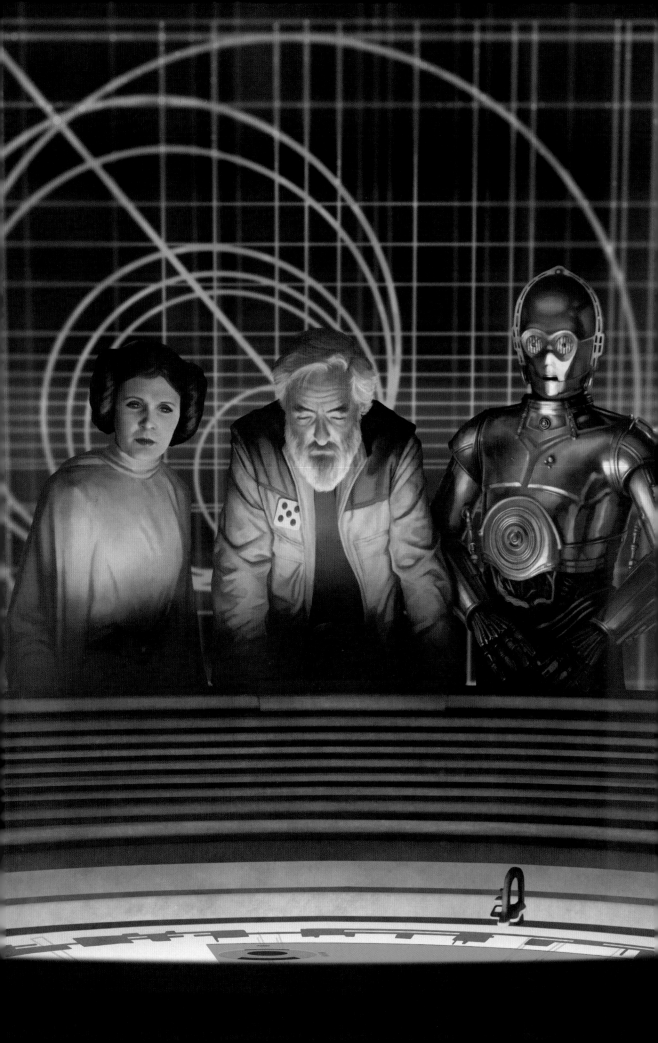

"MAN YOUR SHIPS—
AND MAY THE FORCE BE WITH YOU."
— GENERAL DODONNA

As the Death Star hones in on the *Falcon*, the rebel pilots ready their
X-wing starfighters and prepare to risk their lives for their cause.

GGS—I TOLD YOU I'D MAKE IT SO

— LUKE SKYWALKER

up for the battle, Luke shares a happy reunion with his old
atooine, Biggs Darklighter. The two look forward to flying tog
t like old times—only now, they won't be shooting womp ra
They'll be fighting the Empire.

"WHAT GOOD'S A REWARD IF YOU AIN'T AROUND TO USE IT?" — HAN SOLO

But one good pilot has other things on his mind: getting as far away as possible with the reward he was promised. Han has debts to pay, and no interest in a suicide mission—no matter what Luke or Chewbacca have to say about it.

STAR WARS: JEDI OF THE REPUBLIC — MACE WINDU #4 **WILL SLINEY** & **RACHELLE ROSENBERG**

"LUKE...TRUST YOUR FEELINGS."
— OBI-WAN KENOBI

Accompanied by the ever-faithful R2-D2, Luke takes flight as Red Five as the rebels begin their assault on the fast-approaching Death Star, scant minutes away from firing range. Only one courageous pilot needs to get close enough to fire the crucial proton torpedo—but barring the way are the Empire's deadly surface canons and a fleet of TIE fighters. In his head, Luke hears the voice of his old friend, Obi-Wan Kenobi, guiding him in his attack on the Death Star's surface.

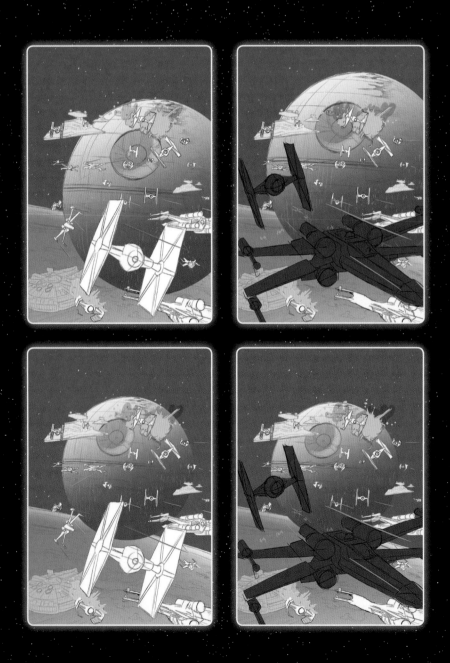

STAR WARS: POE DAMERON #21 **ASHLEY WITTER**

"I'LL TAKE THEM MYSELF—COVER ME."
— DARTH VADER

Flanked by a pair of elite pilots, Vader enters the fray and swiftly destroys several of Gold Squadron's Y-wings and Red Squadron's X-wings. But with the Death Star bearing down on Yavin 4, Red Leader manages to launch his proton torpedo at the crucial exhaust port. It strikes the surface, but fails to hit the target. Instead, Vader shoots down Red Leader.

The Death Star is in range of the rebel base, and Tarkin gives the order to fire when ready. The Rebellion has only one chance for survival—but Luke has turned off his targeting computer, and R2-D2 was damaged in the firefight. Now relying solely on his own instincts, and with mere seconds to spare, Luke takes his fateful shot at the exhaust port...

STAR WARS (2015) #40 **DANIEL WARREN JOHNSON** & **MIKE SPICER**

...and the Death Star explodes! As Luke flies clear, Vader's TIE fighter is sent spinning off into space—and the rebel celebration can begin.

THE DESTRUCTION OF THE DEATH STAR IN *STAR WARS* (1977) #6 • ART BY **HOWARD CHAYKIN, BILL WRAY, RICK HOBERG** & **PATY COCKRUM**

STAR WARS: POE DAMERON #22 **MIKE DEL MUNDO**

> ## "REMEMBER, THE FORCE WILL BE WITH YOU, ALWAYS." — OBI-WAN KENOBI

With Obi-Wan's words in his head, Luke has begun his long and difficult journey toward his destiny as a Jedi. He has lost much, and even greater hardships lie ahead—but now is a time for joy. With a gleaming C-3PO and a repaired R2-D2 looking on, the heroes of the Rebellion—Luke, Han and Chewbacca—are honored in a special ceremony in the packed throne room of Yavin 4's Massassi temple, where Princess Leia herself bestows the medals. Together, they have struck a major blow to the Empire—and brought new hope to the galaxy.

THE GUARDIANS OF THE GALAXY FAR, FAR AWAY

Marvel's *Star Wars* editor, Jordan D. White, talks 40 years of *A New Hope* with the two writers tasked with continuing the saga in comic-book form: Jason Aaron, who launched the *Star Wars* title in 2015 and scripted the first 37 issues; and Kieron Gillen, who follows runs on *Darth Vader* and its follow-up series, *Star Wars: Doctor Aphra*, by taking over the flagship book with issue #38. Together they share their favorites of the 40th Anniversary Variant Covers—and discuss the joy of *Star Wars* storytelling.

JORDAN D. WHITE: I was negative 2 years old when the original *Star Wars* hit the screens in 1977, so obviously I didn't see it in theaters. In fact, I cannot remember the first time I saw the movie we now call *A New Hope*—it's just always been a part of my life. The knowledge of Luke Skywalker, Princess Leia, et al. is buried all the way back there in my memory with the knowledge of my family members and the alphabet. The fact that I now get to oversee the creation of all-new stories about these massive, mythical characters is one of the most amazing parts of my job, and one I am ever grateful for. So as the 40th anniversary of the film that started it all came closer, we knew we had to celebrate.

And I knew I wasn't the only one who would want to. Since I started on the *Star Wars* comics, I've heard from countless of Marvel's greatest artists how much they love it and

cannot wait for their chance to leave their mark on the galaxy far, far away. That's how I hit on the idea for what you hold in your hands: We break the story of *A New Hope* into 48 distinct images and release those as variant covers all across the anniversary year, four per month, and each with a different artist. Marvel's top artists joining together to retell one of the most important stories in modern pop culture.

My assistant editor, Heather Antos, and I made up the list of moments from the film, and then Heather took point on reaching out to the artists and coordinating the schedule. We couldn't be happier with the results, and we hope you'll agree. We ALSO hope that Jason Aaron and Kieron Gillen are happy with them, as they join us here to discuss the covers and the legacy of *A New Hope*.

Welcome, guys! Let's start with our tribute to

STAR WARS: ROGUE ONE ADAPTATION #1 COVER BY **MIKE MAYHEW**

the film. What is your favorite scene from *A New Hope*? And how do you feel the corresponding cover captured it?

KIERON GILLEN: Oh, man. What's your favorite is just the hardest. It's *A New Hope*—it's this greatest-hit string of iconic beats and scenes and moments. You'd get a different favorite if you asked me at every different mood. You ask me when I've got my craft nerd head on, and I'd nod at the opening shot of the cantina, which is a masterclass in world-building and mood. Hey—here's a bunch of weird-looking aliens, chilling, but threateningly so. You've got more imagination in each individual alien than most science-fiction movies made today.

And Mike Mayhew's take goes a different way than just "here is a world on the page." You get the photo-realistic vibe, and the band playing, whatever that alien is called on the dance floor throwing down and spilling its drink while Jawas look on as if they're Baby left in the corner. It's not drawing the scene but imagining something that could easily happen in that bar. That's a really fun approach.

JASON AARON: By far my favorite part of *A New Hope*, when everything completely clicks for me, is when Han and Luke rescue Leia. That's when the bickering goes up to 11. And I love every second of it. They're all blundering their way through what appears to be a hopeless rescue mission, and they all seem to be incredibly annoyed by one another. That to me is at the heart of *Star Wars* and why I first fell in love with this ragtag band of rebels. We fall in love with those characters before they ever fall in love with each other. The story earns that love and respect, by putting them all through hell together. And one of the best and most memorable examples of that hell is the trash-compactor scene, which is perfectly captured here by the amazing Tradd Moore and Matthew Wilson. The bending rod. Luke's intensity as he's yelling into the communicator at C-3PO.

STAR WARS: POE DAMERON #18 COVER BY
TRADD MOORE & **MATTHEW WILSON**

The hint of the monster lurking below. It's all there. Never has a room full of wet garbage looked so beautiful. Or like so much fun.

JORDAN: You heard it here first, folks—Jason Aaron calls Marvel's *Star Wars* comics wet garbage. Sorry, sorry, just doing that annoyed-bickering thing you like so much. Speaking of things you like so much, which cover is your favorite of the 48?

KIERON: Jordan, you know that asking me my favorite of 48 is a surefire way to make 47 artists want to fire a proton torpedo down my exhaust pipe, right? I haven't survived in this industry by making enemies like that.

Okay. I'll select a couple. Stephanie Hans' take on the death of Alderaan solves the storytelling problem to maximize the emotion. The problem being, we need to see Alderaan being destroyed. We also need to see Leia's face to capture the anguish. So Stephanie uses the reflection in the Death Star bridge to show the chaos, and then uses the composition to capture the pain of the princess. That's great stuff. Oh, and Daniel Acuña's storming of Leia's prison is just a joy. So much energy, so much color.

STAR WARS (2015) #37 COVER BY **GREG SMALLWOOD**

an interesting one. Rather than drawing what the scene looks like, or a take on the emotions of it, it draws the whole section in a single image. It's actually a very comic-cover image, rather than a realistic image. Clearly, Han and Chewie weren't actually excitedly counting their reward directly at the back of the briefing...but that's the point of that section of *A New Hope*, and it captures all of that.

JASON: Yeah, that's a great way to sum up that moment in time for Han. I'm also really struck by the cover of Vader standing over Ben Kenobi's empty cloak by Greg Smallwood. It's a very stark image, but it manages to feel quite somber and sad to me, and gives a real gravitas to the climax of that long-running Obi-Wan/Anakin relationship.

JORDAN: I was really blown away by Julian Totino Tedesco's depiction of Ben Kenobi sensing the destruction of Alderaan. It's such a quiet moment in the film, but a powerful one, and the way he depicted it put all that power and explosiveness into an image of a calm older gentleman. It really shows his oneness with the Force. I mean Kenobi's, not Tedesco's...but both, I guess.

This movie made such an impact on so many people—and I assume on each of us—what's it like to be able to literally continue the story from such a huge saga right where it left off when you were a kid?

JASON: Yeah, Acuña's cover is one of my faves as well. So is the other cover of Leia's rescue, by Amy Reeder, where she grabs a blaster and joins in, much to the surprise of the boys. I also love the cover by Daniel Warren Johnson and Mike Spicer of Luke's X-wing as it's making that fateful, final shot to destroy the Death Star. That's a very kinetic moment that feels very active and alive, but at the same time you can also somehow feel your heart stuck in your throat, like you're frozen, waiting to see if those torpedoes actually make it into that exhaust port.

JORDAN: Those are really great choices. Another I really love is Ed McGuinness, Mark Morales and Laura Martin's image of Han and Chewie fighting their way off the Death Star. I think they really nailed the roaring energy of Chewbacca and the cocky certitude of that scoundrel Han. Great-looking cover. Are there any that really surprised you, or went a different way with the image than you would have expected?

KIERON: Oh, a bunch. Will Sliney and Jordan Boyd's take on the Death Star briefing is

KIERON: I talked a little about this when taking over *Darth Vader*, but *The Empire Strikes Back* was the first movie I remember seeing in the cinema. Vader was my first image of evil, the movie my founding myth. That I got to write the prologue to my own entrance into geek culture is the sort of inspired meta lunacy that sounds like a "Grant Morrison writes *The Terminator*" setup. If you squint.

So the more amazing thing is how my brain hasn't just fried over the whole thing. In fact, writing in the *Star Wars* universe is incredibly natural. It's fast and comes from the gut, and while I'm aware I should be paralyzed with doubt, I just feel entirely free.

Clearly, I suspect I'm in denial about it, and it'll sink in in a few years' time, and I'll have to lie down and cry for a while.

JASON: It was a huge honor and a thrill, of course, and I'm really proud of what I was able to accomplish over 37 issues. In the beginning, when we first started working on these comics, we all talked about wanting them to feel like the films, right? To feel like an extension of that original trilogy. Like the next chapter of that story, one that you just couldn't skip. And I feel like we all did a good job of that. I'm really happy about all the big moments we were able to include— like Luke facing Vader, Luke fighting Boba Fett, Vader learning that Luke is his son and [readers] finding out that Han has a "wife."

JORDAN: Since we're talking about it... Jason, how does it feel to put those toys down now, as you leave the series? And Kieron, any thoughts on picking things up right where Jason left them?

JASON: Well, I definitely wasn't bored or tired of writing those characters. I totally could've stuck around and not run out of ideas. But I feel like that's also what made it a good time to step away. Better to leave when you've still got some bullets left in your holster than when you've fired them all. Just means that someday maybe I'll have to come back and write some of these folks again. But for now, I'm just excited to see what Kieron is gonna do. I've loved everything he's done in *Star Wars*–land so far, so I don't expect this to be any different. Maybe just with fewer murder droids.

KIERON: I'm still not sure that Jason isn't going to go "PSYCH!" and carry on writing it. Assuming this isn't all some elaborate Aaronian practical joke, there's a completely different set of pressures. Jason and his collaborators have done so much with the book, and I have to find a way to approach the material and find meaningful adventures for all the cast in the period. I think I've got that—this is a militaristic, rebel-centric *Rogue One*-y book as opposed to the core-Jedi approach that Jason leaned toward—but I just hope we can pull it off. Luckily, it's post–*A New Hope*, so there's lots of hope to go around. Hope for everyone!

JORDAN: One more question, just because I am interested: When you talk about this film, do you usually call it *A New Hope*, Episode IV or *Star Wars*? I admit—in my heart of hearts, I can never really stop thinking of it as just *Star Wars*.

KIERON: Yeah, me, too. I will shamefully admit to having to explicitly stop, take a half breath and then say *A New Hope* rather than just saying *Star Wars*. Let's hope this doesn't get me fired.

JASON: Ha, yeah, I'm totally the same. Saying *A New Hope* always feels a little to me like when we were all referring to Prince as "The Artist Formerly Known as Prince." He will always be Prince to me (may he rest in peace)—and *Star Wars* will always be *Star Wars*.

STAR WARS: DARTH MAUL (2017) #5 COVER BY **JULIAN TOTINO TEDESCO**

HOW TO DRAW *STAR WARS* THE MARVEL WAY

Heather Antos, Terry Dodson, Stephanie Hans, Mike Mayhew and Will Sliney share insights into the process of bringing the 40th Anniversary Variant Cover program to life.

So the idea had been to retell *Star Wars: Episode IV A New Hope* via the artistic medium of the comic-book cover. But how do you go about turning that vision into reality? For Marvel's *Star Wars* assistant editor, Heather Antos, the process naturally began by spending a couple of hours in the company of an old friend: the original movie. "It was pretty easy, really," Antos confesses. "When I got the assignment, I knew already how many scenes the story had to be broken down into. So it was basically as simple as going home, popping in the DVD with a notebook in hand and just jotting down the key events as the film progressed. After I finished watching, I counted up the scenes and then had to decide which moments needed to be cut, or expanded upon, to fit 48 covers." Simple as that. She only had to watch the film once—largely because, as she puts it, "I've had that movie basically memorized for years now! Some of my earliest memories of my childhood are playing 'escape the trash compactor' on my elementary school's playground!"

If step one was child's play, the next—recruiting the talent to bring each cover to life—was fairly straightforward, too. After all, finding comic-book artists with a passion for *Star Wars* isn't too hard. "When the project got officially announced at the end of 2016, I had a few artists reach out to me via Twitter campaigns for specific moments and scenes," Antos says. "Specifically, I remember Chip Zdarsky pleading for the Han/Jabba scene on Tatooine. I hadn't cast that scene yet, and everyone loves a good Chip Zdarsky cover, so I emailed him straightaway. It just goes to show if you want something, it never hurts to ask!"

Editorial input into the approach to each cover varied, depending on the artist and particular scene involved. "There are some artists that are just *beyond* when it comes to coming up with cover designs," Antos says, "so I didn't want to give them any direction whatsoever. I wanted to see what they came up with. I think the most exciting part of this project has been seeing how these scenes, both famous and infamous, have been reinterpreted. It's very cool seeing them through different lenses—a different place in the galaxy at that moment, through a different character's eyes." And indeed, different creators' eyes. With so many glorious images to choose from, which would Antos most like to hang on her wall? "Hands down the cover that stands out to me is Julian Totino Tedesco's Ben Kenobi/Alderaan 'I feel a great disturbance in the Force' cover that appeared on *Star Wars: Darth Maul #5*. It completely takes my breath away and totally captures that moment in a way that the film just can't. You really get a sense that Ben is feeling Alderaan's destruction through the Force. And in a way, the viewer now does, too."

Another standout cover is unique in the use of a word balloon: Kevin Nowlan's "These aren't the droids you're looking for" piece for *Star Wars (2015) #31*. "He was actually the only artist who suggested using one," Antos says. "Gives it a very old-school look, which is really fun!"

But few creators could have been more enthusiastic for the project than Will Sliney (*Fearless Defenders*, *Spider-Man 2099*). "I'm a huge fan of it all," Sliney says of *Star Wars*. "The films, the comics, the animated series, the art books and—unfortunately for my bank account—the Hot Toys. Most of all, though, I love the idea that a single story idea has sparked a universe that so many people have created stories in, whether it's kids playing out imaginary scenarios with their toys or the many great *Star Wars* stories that are being told today."

Sliney isn't alone in being unable to remember when he first saw *A New Hope*—it was released before he was born—but he does recall seeing *The Empire Strikes Back* for the first time: "Funnily enough, my mom went to the video rental store (remember those?) and picked up *Empire*, but I thought I had already seen it as I just saw *Star Wars* on the cover. It blew my mind. I do remember going to the cinema for the re-releases, though."

Sliney's cover for *Star Wars: Jedi of the Republic—Mace Windu #4* required him to tackle the key scene in which Han Solo turns his back on the Rebellion, choosing instead to take his reward and run—and the artist worked through a number of different ways of depicting it. What influenced his approach? "Well, two things really," he says. "I wanted to get across the boldness of Han as he was convincing himself that taking the money and leaving was the right thing to do. I also wanted to cram in as much *Star Wars* as I could, so I played with a few of the characters that surrounded Han in that scene, whether it was Biggs meeting Luke, Leia being disappointed in Han leaving, or just the hustle and bustle of that scene. In the end, I got my wish and really got to pack in a lot of characters in that image. A lot of funky hairdos, too."

As part of his design process, Sliney worked up a number of head sketches for key figures in the scene, demonstrating his skill at capturing the spirit of these instantly recognizable characters—and, yes, their funky hairdos.

So what's his secret? "I've worked on tons of likeness comics over the years," he says. "I always find that you have to mix the right amount of cartooning into your likenesses, to stop it going too photo-real. Once you cross that line, it's easier to throw down one line of ink that can take the likeness down the wrong direction. For some reason, and a lot of artists will agree with me, Han, Luke and Leia are three of the hardest likenesses to draw out there. But once you bring your own style of art and mix it in with their features, when you get the right balance it comes across well on the page."

Does he have a particular favorite to draw? "All of them!" he jokes. "Nah, it is very hard to choose. My favorite character is Obi-Wan, but I really like the challenge of drawing Luke or Anakin, etc. I can draw Darth Vader with my eyes closed, the amount of times I have doodled that mask just in my own spare time."

Another talented artist who seemingly has no problem capturing that iconic helmet is Stephanie Hans (*Journey Into Mystery*, *Angela: Asgard's Assassin*). The Dark Lord of the Sith features in her own variant cover, portraying the pivotal scene in which the Death Star destroys Alderaan. Faced with the challenge of capturing that cataclysmic moment, as well as Princess Leia's anguished reaction, Hans employed a clever approach to layout for her final piece, gracing *Star Wars: Poe Dameron #16*.

"The difficulty in this scene is the scale of the scene," she says. "You have to include the Death Star, Alderaan and the characters involved—and at the same time, put in the emotion. Leia is a princess, she has to have some presence, even in despair, and Vader is her father, even if they are unaware at that moment. I wanted to convey the cruelty of it all."

Asked to rank her *Star Wars* fandom on a scale of 1–10, Hans replies: "I don't know, 12?" She clearly remembers seeing *A New Hope* for the first time as a young girl, growing up in Strasbourg, France, where she watched the original version subtitled. "Life was giving me a hard time at that moment," she recalls, "and it gave me a small bubble where I could forget about it and be an awkward kid all over again, for a couple of hours. Much appreciated. Being a part of the *Star Wars* universe now, even to this modest extent, is entering pop-culture history. I am always amazed that I am asked to contribute to creations that built the artist I am today. I think, for an illustrator, it is one of the greatest achievements."

Fan-favorite penciler Terry Dodson (*Marvel Knights Spider-Man, Uncanny X-Men*) was at the perfect age of 7 when *A New Hope* came out, and he describes himself as a bigger fan of *Star Wars* than he is even of Marvel super heroes. As a result, he was excited to take part in the 40th Anniversary Variant Cover program. "My mind started racing to think of my single favorite moment—and there were so many!" he says. When it came down to it, Dodson took on the scene in which Luke and his uncle acquire C-3PO and R2-D2 from the Jawas—on *Star Wars: Darth Maul (2017) #1*—and he, too, considered more than one way of translating the sequence into a single image. "It really came down to telling the most obvious story first," he says, "which led me pretty quickly to this design, knowing I could fit in everything else in the background. I threw in a couple of extras, figuring I might as well squeeze as much as possible in."

Dodson—and his wife and artistic partner, inker Rachel Dodson—are known for their heroic women, which made them ideal to illustrate Marvel's *Princess Leia* series. But they are equally at home with male characters— as demonstrated on their variant cover to *Star Wars (2015) #24* featuring Chewbacca and Han Solo, the latter in a certain stolen costume from a memorable scene from *A New Hope*. "All the classic *Star Wars* characters I love—it's so much fun to draw them. And the issue #24 cover was by my request—it was supposed to be a series of stormtrooper covers and I thought, 'Heck, I love Han and Luke in those outfits—let's do that instead!'"

For Dodson, the key to convincing *Star Wars* artwork is staying true to the characters: "It really is their attitude, their defining action for that particular expression—each of those characters really act a particular way for each shot." But if Marvel follows suit with a similar variant-cover celebration for the 40th anniversary of *The Empire Strikes Back*, facial expressions won't be an issue, should Dodson get his way. Asked what scene he would select, he's adamant: "Gotta be something with Boba Fett!" Mike Mayhew (*Avengers, The Star Wars*)

STAR WARS: POE DAMERON #16 COVER BY **STEPHANIE HANS**

was the same age as Dodson when *A New Hope* hit the silver screen. "I was the prime audience for it," he recalls, "raised on *Planet of the Apes, Famous Monsters of Filmland* magazine and *Star Trek. Star Wars* pretty much blew my mind. I first saw it with my best bud from second grade and his dad at the Cine Capri theater in Phoenix, Arizona. That was the best theater, with the biggest screen in the state. I will never forget it."

And through the years, Mayhew says he has only grown more appreciative: "I'm a huge admirer of the risk George Lucas took and the tenacity he had when making the first movie, and I'm in awe of his business acumen. I've grown to love the prequels. I have a 9-year-old, and Anakin from Episodes II and III is his man. He loves those ones the best, and I see them through his eyes."

For Mayhew himself, though, Luke will always be the star: "There is something about his '70s hair, blue eyes and farmboy looks that screams *Star Wars*. Drawing the original characters for me is like playing with my old Kenner action figures—I could lose myself in their adventures."

While it doesn't feature Luke, Mayhew's cover for *Star Wars: Rogue One Adaptation #1* boasts a hard-to-beat cast: the Mos Eisley cantina band! Depicting that scene must surely have had the infectious John Williams score running through his head for weeks. "I did think of the music!" he says. "My mentality was, if you saw the art and didn't hum the tune, it was a failure!"

The artist has shared almost his whole life with *Star Wars*: "Of course, everyone always asks me if I'm related to Peter Mayhew, who played Chewbacca—I did tell kids in elementary school he was my uncle!" But he had, pardon the pun, lost all hope of working on the franchise himself—until a unique opportunity presented itself in 2013. "I had written off *Star Wars*," he says, "until one day out of the blue I got this email from Dark Horse Comics to draw

STAR WARS: DARTH MAUL (2017) #1 COVER BY
TERRY DODSON & RACHEL DODSON

The Star Wars. Honestly, that morning I was in the shower thinking about the new *Star Wars* movie J.J. Abrams was going to make. I was so jealous/fascinated with the task J.J. had in front of him. I remember thinking to myself in the shower, if I got the call to help make a new *Star Wars*, I would say, 'Guys...I've been waiting to hear from you since I was 7 years old.' I went in the office and was blown away at the email waiting for me, which was basically a chance to remake *Star Wars* via George's original, largely unknown draft. And I've been drawing *Star Wars* ever since."

Indeed he has—not least with interior artwork on Marvel's *Star Wars* series, in which he has demonstrated a flair for illustrating the past adventures of a younger Obi-Wan Kenobi. In addition, Mayhew's ever-eye-catching covers have graced that and related books, as he joins an incredible roster of talents whose works of art are as suited to hanging in museums as adorning the fronts of comic books.

Over the following pages, we have selected some of the finest covers from Marvel's various *Star Wars* titles, each featuring the iconic cast of *A New Hope*—including pieces by Mayhew and Dodson, as well as John Cassaday, Joe Quesada, Alex Ross, Skottie Young and more. We hope you'll agree that the Force is strong in this gallery.

JOURNEY TO STAR WARS: THE FORCE AWAKENS — SHATTERED EMPIRE #1 VARIANT COVER BY **MIKE MAYHEW**

STAR WARS (2015) #8 VARIANT COVER BY **JOHN CASSADAY** & **LAURA MARTIN**

STAR WARS (2015) #8 COVER BY **STUART IMMONEN**, **WADE VON GRAWBADGER** & **JUSTIN PONSOR**

STAR WARS (2015) #12 COVER BY **STUART IMMONEN**, **WADE VON GRAWBADGER** & **JUSTIN PONSOR**

STAR WARS (2015) #17 COVER BY **TERRY DODSON** & **RACHEL DODSON**

STAR WARS (2015) #17 VARIANT COVER BY **LEINIL FRANCIS YU**

STAR WARS ANNUAL #2 COVER BY **MIKE MAYHEW**

STAR WARS (2015) #16 VARIANT COVER BY **FRANCESCO FRANCAVILLA**

STAR WARS (2015) #17 VARIANT COVER BY **FRANCESCO FRANCAVILLA**

STAR WARS (2015) #24 VARIANT COVER BY **TERRY DODSON** & **RACHEL DODSON**

HAN SOLO #1 COVER BY **LEE BERMEJO**

HAN SOLO #1 VARIANT COVER BY **JOHN CASSADAY** & **PAUL MOUNTS**

HAN SOLO #1 VARIANT COVER BY **MICHAEL ALLRED** *&* **LAURA ALLRED**

HAN SOLO #2 COVER BY **TULA LOTAY**

CHEWBACCA #1 VARIANT COVER BY **ALEX ROSS**

STAR WARS (2015) #7 COVER BY **JOHN CASSADAY** & **LAURA MARTIN**

STAR WARS (2015) #7 VARIANT COVER BY **SIMONE BIANCHI**

STAR WARS (2015) #15 COVER BY **MIKE MAYHEW**

STAR WARS (2015) #36 COVER BY **MIKE MAYHEW**

DARTH VADER (2015) *#15* VARIANT COVER BY **FRANCESCO FRANCAVILLA**

DARTH VADER (2015) #9 VARIANT COVER BY **ADI GRANOV**

DARTH VADER (2015) *#13* COVER BY **MARK BROOKS**

DARTH VADER (2015) #16 COVER BY **KAARE ANDREWS**

DARTH VADER (2015) #17 COVER BY **KAARE ANDREWS**

DARTH VADER (2015) #25 COVER BY **JUAN GIMÉNEZ**

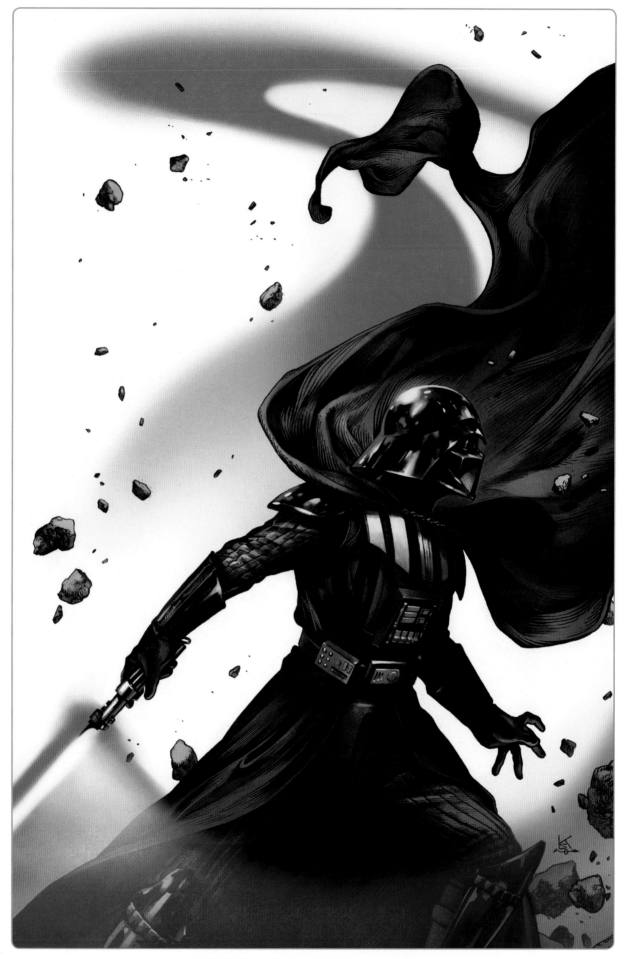

DARTH VADER (2015) #25 VARIANT COVER BY **KAMOME SHIRAHAMA**

DARTH VADER (2015) #25 VARIANT COVER BY **CHRIS SAMNEE** & **MATTHEW WILSON**

DARTH VADER (2015) #25 VARIANT COVER BY **JOE QUESADA** & **RICHARD ISANOVE**

DARTH VADER (2017) *#1 VARIANT COVER BY* **ADI GRANOV**

DARTH VADER (2017) #1 VARIANT COVER BY **FRANCESCO MATTINA**

THE GREATEST SPACE-FANTASY OF ALL!

It may have been cover dated July 1977, but Marvel's original *Star Wars #1* actually hit shelves ahead of the film's May 25, 1977, release—and so offered eager comic-book fans their first look at Luke Skywalker, Princess Leia, Han Solo, C-3PO, R2-D2, Obi-Wan Kenobi and the fearsome Darth Vader. The issue began a six-chapter adaptation of *Star Wars: Episode IV A New Hope* by writer Roy Thomas and artist Howard Chaykin, which presented all the classic scenes in the "Mighty Marvel Manner"—as well as a few that never made it to cinema screens. *Star Wars #1*, reprinted in full here, began a hugely successful 107-issue run now available in its entirety in three *Star Wars: The Original Marvel Years* Omnibus volumes. In place of a letters page, the book offered the following essay by Thomas on how *Star Wars* arrived at the House of Ideas.

STAR WARRIORS

℅ MARVEL COMICS GROUP, 575 MADISON AVE. N.Y.C. 10022

THE STORY BEHIND *STAR WARS*
The Movie and the Comic-Mag
by Roy Thomas

It started slowly, this *Star Wars* project. Both for George Lucas and even for Marvel Comics.

It's a couple of years now since I met George Lucas, already celebrated as the film-maker behind the blockbuster *American Graffiti*. I was an ardent admirer of that film (and had also been intrigued by his earlier, science-fiction feature *ThX 1138*). George, in turn, had expressed a desire to see the Carl Barks/ Uncle Scrooge McDuck painting which hangs proudly in my living room, and was enthusiastic about another pride and joy of mine, our late lamented $1 magazine UNKNOWN WORLDS OF SCIENCE FICTION. We met, shared a dinner and a few anecdotes, and that was it.

Or so it seemed.

For, a few months later, a friend of George's looked me up. His name was Charlie Lippincott, and he was (for lack of a better term, he said) media projects director of George Lucas' new film, *Star Wars*, about which I knew nothing but the name.

Fairly understandable, since at that stage filming hadn't even been started.

Charlie informed me, after a spaghetti dinner and some more swapped anecdotes, that he and George would like Marvel Comics in general and me in particular to handle the comic-book adaptation of *Star Wars*. I was, of course, both flattered and flabbergasted. And, when Charlie brought out stats of a dozen or so beautiful paintings of projected scenes from the movie ("sketches," they're called in the trade, but they were painstakingly detailed and breathtakingly beautiful), I was definitely hooked.

Within a couple of days, Smilin' Stan Lee had seen my enthusiasm and figured, I guess, that "What the heck, it'll give the Kid something to do." STAR WARS was tentatively added to the hectic Marvel schedule, after some slight debate about whether it should be a color or black-and-white mag, about whether it should be adapted in one issue or twenty, etc. I wanted to adapt George's script in about a half dozen issues, in full color—and I guess I was fairly persuasive that particular day.

By that time, reading over the script and having perused the illustrations which would soon become filmic reality, I had already chosen the artist I would give first crack at STAR-WARS, Marvel version.

Howard Chaykin's drawn space fantasy (or space opera, if you will) for just about every market over the past couple of years. For our competition, for underground-type mags, and even for *us*, as witness last year's MARVEL PREMIERE issue featuring one MONARK STARSTALKER. Howie took one look at the script and the "production sketches," and his only question was—"When do we start?"

He's got top-notch help, too, to help the two of us produce the STAR WARS comic on a monthly basis. This issue's cover, for instance, based on a poster by the talented Mr. C., was inked by Tom Palmer, a favorite of Marveldom Assembled. And, starting with issue #2, the inking chores (if you can call such an enjoyable assignment a "chore") will be done by Steve Leialoha, in between encounters with HOWARD THE DUCK. We think Chaykin and Leialoha are gonna be a duo to remember.

And STAR WARS, both as film and as comic-book, is going to be just what it says out there on the **first page**:

"The Greatest Space-Fantasy of All!"

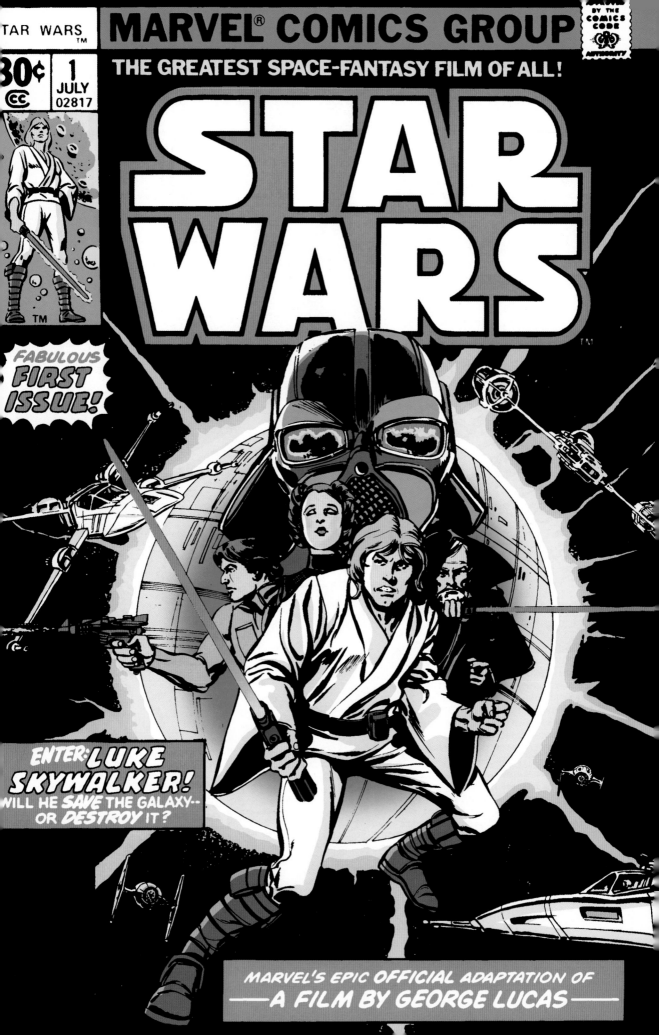

Stan Lee PRESENTS: ROY THOMAS SCRIPTER/EDITOR ★ HOWARD CHAYKIN ILLUSTRATOR ★ JIM NOVAK LETTERER ★ ...ADAPTING THE GREATEST SPACE-FANTASY OF ALL!

STAR WARS

ADAPTED FROM THE GEORGE LUCAS FILM

It is a period of CIVIL WAR in the galaxy.

A brave alliance of UNDERGROUND FREEDOM FIGHTERS has challenged the tyranny and oppression of the awesome GALACTIC EMPIRE.

To CRUSH the rebellion once and for all, the EMPIRE is constructing a sinister new BATTLE STATION. Powerful enough to destroy an entire planet, its COMPLETION will spell CERTAIN DOOM for the champions of freedom.

Striking from a fortress hidden among the billion stars of the galaxy, REBEL SPACESHIPS have won their first victory in a battle with the powerful IMPERIAL STARFLEET. The Empire fears that ANOTHER defeat could bring a THOUSAND MORE solar systems into the rebellion, and IMPERIAL CONTROL over the galaxy would be LOST FOREVER.

BUT, THAT IS THE NEAR FUTURE.

AT THIS MOMENT:

ABOVE THE YELLOW PLANET TATOOINE, A GIGANTIC IMPERIAL STARSHIP PURSUES A REBEL SPACECRAFT--ITS DEADLY LASER BOLTS DISINTEGRATE THE SMALLER SHIP'S MAIN SOLAR FIN WITH A SOULSEARING SHUDDER...!

MARIE SEVERIN, COLORIST

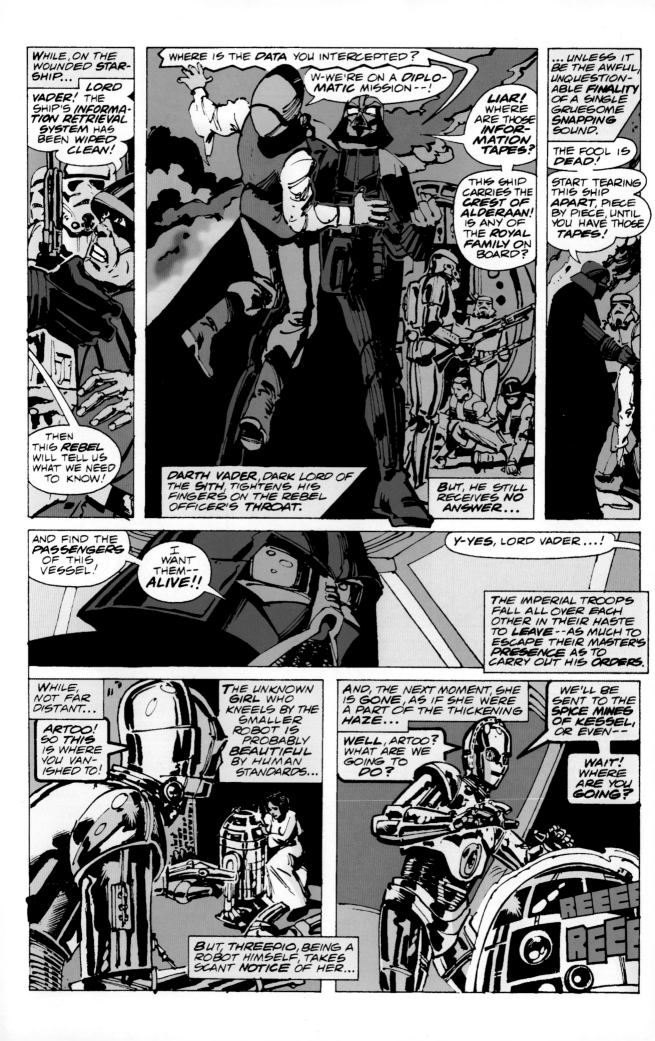

SOON AFTERWARD, AT DINNER...

UNCLE OWEN -- I THINK THAT R2 UNIT MAY BE STOLEN GOODS.

WHAT MAKES YOU THINK *THAT,* LUKE?

THE *DROID* CLAIMS TO BE THE PROPERTY OF SOMEONE CALLED...OBI-WAN KENOBI!

I STUMBLED ON A *RECORDING* WHILE I WAS *CLEANING* HIM...

!

I THOUGHT HE MIGHT MEAN *OLD BEN* -- THE NAME IS SIMILAR. DO YOU KNOW WHAT--?

IT'S A NAME FROM *ANOTHER* TIME, THAT CAN ONLY MEAN *TROUBLE!*

TOMORROW, YOU'LL HAVE THAT R2 UNIT'S *MEMORY* FLUSHED AND THAT'LL BE THE *END* OF IT.

YOU STAY AWAY FROM THAT OLD *WIZARD,* DO YOU HEAR ME? HE'S *DANGEROUS!*

I DON'T CARE *WHERE* THAT DROID CAME FROM; IT BELONGS TO *US* NOW!

BUT, WHAT IF THIS *OBI-WAN* COMES LOOKING FOR THE DROID?

HE WON'T! HE *DIED* AT THE SAME TIME AS YOUR *FATHER.* FORGET ABOUT IT.

DID HE *KNOW* MY FATHER?

I SAID *FORGET* IT!

ALL RIGHT -- BUT IF THESE NEW DROIDS *WORK OUT,* I'D LIKE TO TRANSMIT MY APPLICATION TO THE *ACADEMY* THIS YEAR.

YOU MEAN *NEXT TERM* -- BEFORE THE HARVEST?

YOU'VE GOT *MORE* THAN ENOUGH *DROIDS* TO--

DROIDS CAN'T REPLACE *YOU,* LUKE! IT'S JUST FOR *ONE MORE* SEASON.

FOR THE FIRST TIME, WE'VE GOT A *FORTUNE* COMING INTO OUR HANDS. MAYBE *AFTER* NEXT SEASON...

BUT, THAT MEANS *ANOTHER* YEAR...

THE TIME WILL PASS BEFORE YOU *KNOW* IT.

THAT'S WHAT YOU SAID *LAST* YEAR -- WHEN *BIGGS* AND *TANK* LEFT.

WHERE ARE YOU GOING?

IT LOOKS LIKE I'M GOING *NOWHERE!*

I HAVE TO FINISH CLEANING THOSE *DROIDS.*

OWEN, WE CAN'T KEEP HIM HERE *FOREVER!* MOST OF HIS *FRIENDS* ARE GONE...

I'LL MAKE IT *UP* TO HIM NEXT YEAR ...I *PROMISE.*

LUKE'S JUST *NOT A FARMER,* OWEN. HE'S GOT TOO MUCH OF HIS *FATHER* IN HIM.

THAT'S... WHAT I'M *AFRAID* OF...!

MEANWHILE, SOME DISTANCE AWAY, FOUR IMPERIAL STORMTROOPERS MILL ABOUT A FAMILIAR FORM: A HALF-BURIED LIFE-POD...!

THIS IS THE ONE! BUT, THERE ARE NO DATA TAPES HERE, SIR!

IF ONLY WE KNEW WHO WAS IN THAT POD WHEN IT--

HOLD IT!

THIS SMALL PIECE OF METAL I FOUND IN THE SAND--!

DROIDS!

...OLD BEN KENOBI LIVES OUT IN THIS DIRECTION SOMEWHERE, THREEPIO...

BUT, I DON'T SEE HOW ARTOO COULD HAVE--

AS THE TINY LANDSPEEDER GLIDES ACROSS THE DESERT FLOOR, ITS OCCUPANTS ARE UNAWARE OF A DEADLY LASER RIFLE BEING AIMED AT THEM...

MOMENTS, LATER, FOLLOWING A HEATED ARGUMENT IN THEIR BARBARIC TONGUE, THE TWO SAND-PEOPLE--OR TUSKEN RAIDERS AS THEY'RE SOMETIMES CALLED--ARE SCURRYING OVER THE ROCKY TERRAIN...

...TOWARD THEIR TWO ENORMOUS BANTHAS, TETHERED NEARBY.

MOUNTING THE ELEPHANTINE CREATURES, THEY RIDE OFF DOWN THE RUGGED BLUFF --IN OMINOUS SILENCE.

WAIT! THERE'S SOMETHING DEAD AHEAD ON THE SCANNER!

LOOKS LIKE OUR DROID! HIT IT, THREEPIO!

...AND OF ANOTHER'S HAND, WHICH GRASPS THE GUN BEFORE IT CAN BE FIRED!

A Six-Issue Prospectus On A Startling Piece of Cinema

Six years ago, George Lucas, the creator of *American Graffiti*, began his first draft of the script of a film that is certain to become a milestone in the space fantasy genre.

Thus, it is perhaps appropriate that Marvel Comics is going to take six monthly issues of this STAR WARS comic-magazine to adapt the movie into illustrated form. Anything less than approximately a hundred pages would be too little to do it justice.

Still, just to familiarize you with the territory, including a few terms new to those unfamiliar with interstellar warfare, we thought it'd be best to give you this brief overview of the story, the characters, and the people behind it. Read it carefully, 'cause there might be a quiz at the end of the sixth issue:

Through thousands of light-years come the amazing exploits of hero Luke Skywalker and his friends, flesh-and-blood space pilots and mechanical robots, as they battle numerous villains and creatures in a massive Galactic Civil War. This story has no relationship to Earth time and space. It occurs in other solar systems in another galaxy and could be happening in the future, the past, or even the present.

Young Luke Skywalker is accompanied by his robot companions R2-D2 and C-3PO (more familiarly known as Artoo and Threepio)—the tough starpilot Han Solo—the seven-foot, fur-covered Wookiee named Chewbacca—and the venerable old warrior, Ben Kenobi.

Three different worlds become settings for the series of fabulous adventures and thrills. They travel from the large arid planet Tatooine to the huge man-made planet destroyer, Death Star, and finally arrive on the dense jungle-covered fourth moon of Yavin.

Director/writer George Lucas has created a majestic visual experience of extraordinary worlds. This Panavision Technicolor motion picture, to be released in late May of this year, is produced by Gary Kurtz for Twentieth Century-Fox release and was made on locations in Tunisia and at EMI Elstree and Shepperton Studios, London, over a 17-week schedule.

Lucas and Kurtz, the successful duo of the fantastically popular *American Graffiti*, have acquired an outstanding production team, including production designer John Barry of *A Clockwork Orange* fame and director of photography Gil Taylor of Alfred Hitchcock's *Frenzy* and Twentieth Century-Fox's 1976 hit, *The Omen*. A team with credentials!

John Stears, production special-effects supervisor in London (and Academy Award winner for the James Bond film *Thunderball*) designed the robots and land vehicles and planned the cataclysmic explosions. At a hidden warehouse in the United States, special-effects miniaturist John Dykstra took full advantage of new advances in computer-controlled stop-motion animation. Matte artist Peter Ellenshaw, Jr., carried on a great family tradition in a relatively unknown motion picture art form. John Barry was production designer, while veteran John Williams scored the music.

Other important production members include make-up expert Stuart Freeborn, who designed and made the ape costumes for *2001*, and editors Marcia Lucas, Richard Chew, and Paul Hirsch.

And the *stars* of *Star Wars*?

Sir Alec Guinness stars as Ben (Obi-wan) Kenobi, Mark Hamill as Luke Skywalker, Harrison Ford (a featured player in *Graffiti*) as Han Solo, Carrie Fisher as Princess Leia Organa, and Peter Cushing (of Frankenstein fame and infamy) as Governor Moff Tarkin.

Others in the cast include Anthony Daniels, Kenny Baker, Peter Mayhew, and Dave Prowse—though it's doubtful even their own families would recognize them in their alien get-ups.

Now the question: *"Why* did filmmaker George Lucas follow up a movie like *American Graffiti* with such a totally different film?"

Here's the reason, in his own words:

"I think that anyone who goes to the movies loves to have an emotional experience. It's basic—whether you're seven, seventeen, or seventy. The more intense the experience, the more successful the film.

"I've always loved adventure films. After I finished *American Graffiti*, I came to realize that since the demise of the western, there hasn't been much in the mythological fantasy genre available to the film audience. So, instead of making 'isn't-it-terrible-what's-happening-to-mankind' movies, which is how I began, I decided that I'd try to fill that gap. I'd make a film so rooted in imagination that the grimness of everyday life would not follow the audience into the theatre. In other words, for two hours, they could forget.

"I'm trying to reconstruct a genre that's been lost and bring it to a new dimension so that the elements of space, fantasy, adventure, suspense, and fun all work and feed off each other. So, in a way, *Star Wars* is a movie for the kid in all of us."

With this multi-million-dollar Fox release slated to open in major theatres across the country in just a few short weeks—with a *Star Wars* novelization from Ballantine Books already rushing toward a second printing—and now, with the beginning of Marvel Comics' official adaptation by Roy Thomas (late of UNKNOWN WORLDS OF SCIENCE FICTION and a Skrull/Kree War or two himself) and Howard Chaykin (whose MONARK STARSTALKER and SOLOMON KANE for Marvel have shown he knows how to buckle a mean swash himself, in space or elsewhere)—

—well, it looks as if the time *has* come for STAR WARS, after all!

And it's *about* time!

THE STORY CONTINUES....

START HERE

Star Wars Vol. 1:
Skywalker Strikes
ISBN 978-0-7851-9213-8

Star Wars Vol. 2: Showdown
on the Smuggler's Moon
ISBN 978-0-7851-9214-5

Star Wars:
Vader Down
ISBN 978-0-7851-9789-8

Star Wars Vol. 3:
Rebel Jail
ISBN 978-0-7851-9983-0

Star Wars Vol. 4:
Last Flight of the Harbinger
ISBN 978-0-7851-9984-7

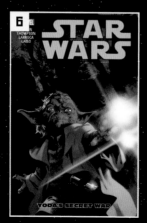

Star Wars Vol. 5:
Yoda's Secret War
ISBN 978-1-302-90265-0

Star Wars:
The Screaming Citadel
ISBN 978-1-302-90678-8

Star Wars Vol. 6:
Out Among the Stars
ISBN 978-1-302-90553-8